Trisha Cain

PewDiePie Calm Coloring Book

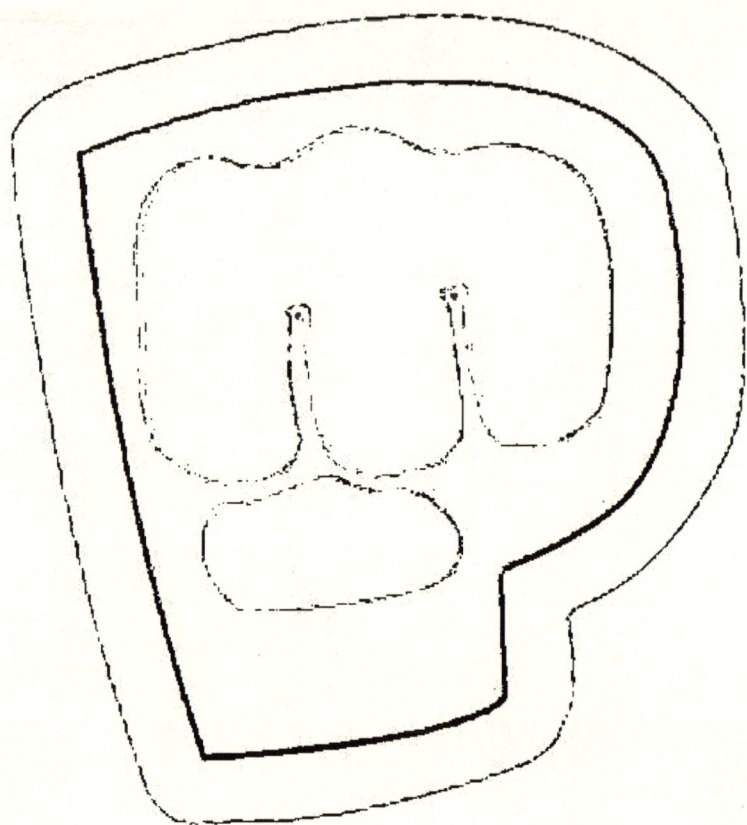

when boys bite their lips

when boys bite your face playfully

when boys leave their
smell on your clothes

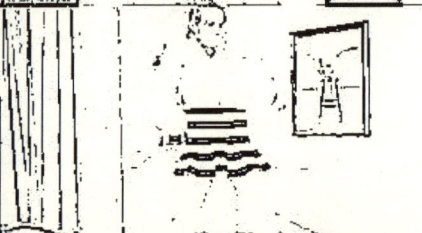

when boys scare you on purpose
to get a reaction

Suprise Bitch!

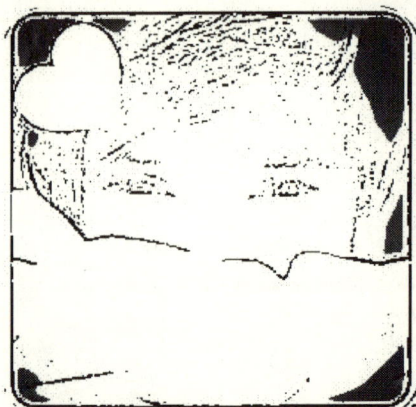

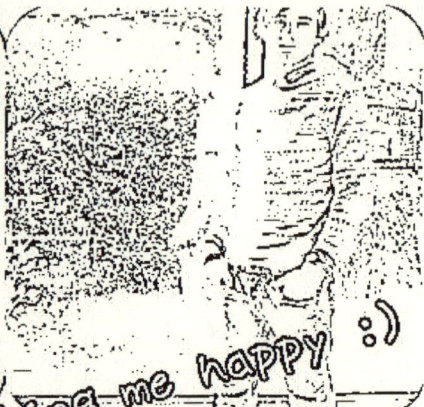

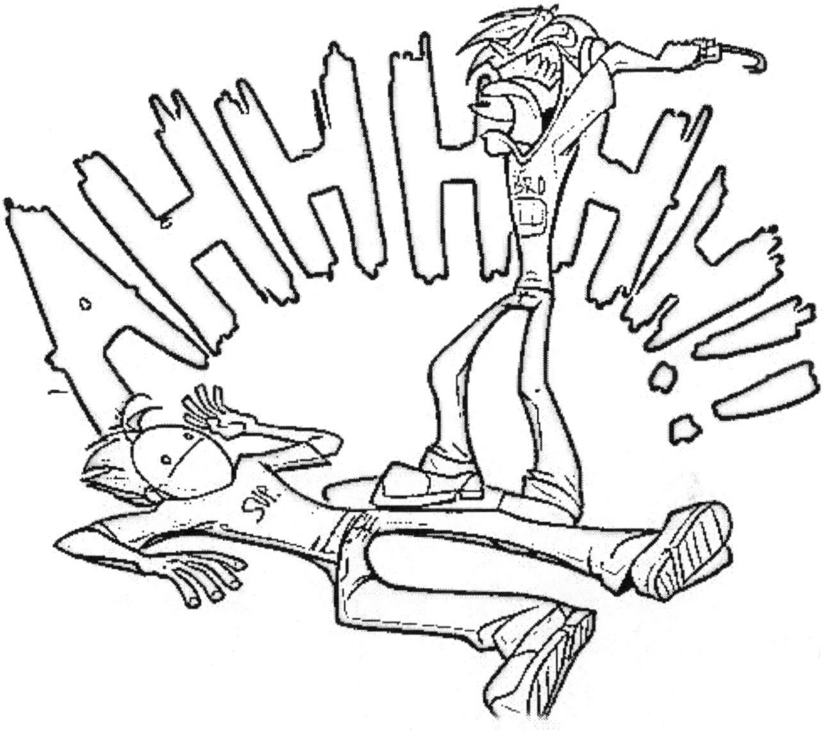
AHHHHH!!
BRO
SIR

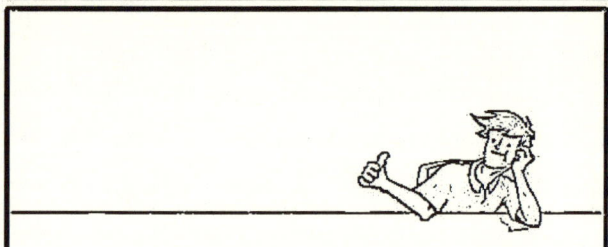

SALAD,

BROCCOLI

ULD
BE!

FELIX KIELBERG

INTERNET BRO FIST

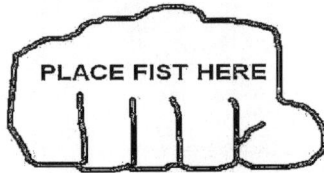

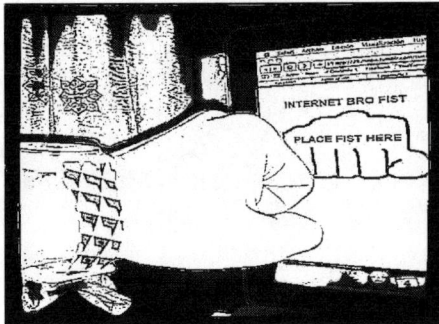

Made in the USA
Monee, IL
21 December 2019